Mystery, So Long

BOOKS BY STEPHEN DOBYNS

Mystery, So Long

Stephen Dobyns

PENGUIN POETS

PENGUIN BOOKS
Published by the Penguin Group
Penguin Group (USA) Inc., 375 Hudson Street, New York, New York 10014, U.S.A.
Penguin Group (Canada), 10 Alcorn Avenue, Toronto, Ontario, Canada M4V 3B2
(a division of Pearson Penguin Canada Inc.)
Penguin Books Ltd, 80 Strand, London WC2R 0RL, England
Penguin Group Ireland, 25 St. Stephen's Green, Dublin 2, Ireland
(a division of Penguin Books Ltd)
Penguin Group (Australia), 250 Camberwell Road, Camberwell, Victoria 3124,
Australia (a division of Pearson Australia Group Pty Ltd)
Penguin Books India Pvt Ltd, 11 Community Centre, Panchsheel Park,
New Delhi – 110 017, India
Penguin Group (NZ), cnr Airborne and Rosedale Roads, Albany, Auckland 1310,
New Zealand (a division of Pearson New Zealand Ltd)
Penguin Books (South Africa) (Pty) Ltd, 24 Sturdee Avenue, Rosebank,
Johannesburg 2196, South Africa

Penguin Books Ltd., Registered Offices:
80 Strand, London WC2R 0RL, England

First published in Penguin Books 2005

10 9 8 7 6 5 4 3 2

Page 97 constitutes an extension to this copyright page.

LIBRARY OF CONGRESS CATALOGING IN PUBLICATION DATA
Dobyns, Stephen, 1941–
Mystery, so long / Stephen Dobyns.
   p.   cm. — (Penguin poets)
ISBN 0 14 30.3462 6
I. Title
PS3554.O2M97 2005
813'.54—dc22   2004063225

Printed in the United States of America
Set in Fruitiger
Designed by Ginger Legato

10 9 8 7 6 5 4 3 2

In memory of
Raj Duvvuri,
Peter Elvins,
Frank Lawson,
Danny Mahoney
and Frank McClendon.

Dentro de poco vas a ofrecer estas páginas a los desconocidos como si extendieras en la mano un manojo de hierbas que tú cortaste.

Ufano y acongojado de tu proeza, regresarás e echarte al rincón preferido.

Dices que eres poeta porque no tienes el pudor necesario del silencio.

¡Bien te vaya, ladrón, con lo que le robas a tu dolor y a tus amores! ¡A ver qué imagen haces de ti mismo con los pedazos que recoges de tu sombra!

—Jaime Sabines

CONTENTS

Mystery, So Long

THE EXIGENCIES OF ART

When a tenor in a too-tight tux begins to sing
Schubert lieder on the stage of a famous hall,
an orangutan in an orange tam-o'-shanter struts

up to the mike, squats at the tenor's feet, takes
a dump, then lopes across the stage and disappears.
In response, the tenor hits half a dozen mistaken

sharps and flats, while the audience of two thousand
feels their attention sideswiped, roller-coastered,
in fact, in two thousand different ways. Bravely,

the tenor yanks his tune back on track and wonders
if he should quickly kick the awful ape offal offstage
with his shiny black wing tip. The pianist considers

halting for a jiffy and hiding the reeking atrocity
under a page of Schubert already successfully sung.
The more serious music lovers see this as a test of art,

that it makes them lift their minds above the humdrum,
in this case five pounds of orangutan splop, and focus
on Schubert's liquid interpolations of tragic themes.

But the fifty kids scattered through the hall all perk up.
A second earlier, they were squirming, complaining,
twiddling their thumbs, tugging their mothers' sleeves,

when something wonderful happened: a champion
marched across the stage and shat. And the music,
which till then had been no more than a jittery tinkling,

a random screech, now takes on heroic proportions,
like Theseus disemboweling the Minotaur, or Icarus
tumbling through the air. Entranced, sitting like statues,

the children wait for the orangutan to reappear
and treat them to another trick—perhaps throw up.
What an awful evening, say the parents later. How

fantastic, say the kids. When can we go back again?
It's hard work to be an artistic entrepreneur, a lover
of beauty, who must not only regale the present crowd,

but seduce a troop of future fans. Like when you pop
the clutch to get an old car moving or a mother puts
a pair of falsies on her skinny daughter, so art at times

requires a kick to get the soul dancing. Late that night
at the stage door, the orangutan drops by for his fifty bucks
and the boss slips him an extra ten for a job well done.

AN ARTIST LIKE ANY OTHER

Let's say a fellow has a little trick—
he can take a rock, toss it about ten feet,

then take another, toss it so it lands on top,
then take a third and toss it on top of that

so all three make a little tower. Each rock
is about the size of a child's fist. Any bigger

or any farther or if he tries a fourth, then
it doesn't work. People are impressed,

but how many times can you watch a guy
do a trick like that? Shortly they wander off.

Children last a little longer. The man's wife
asks to see it once a week just to be nice.

His kids say, Give it a break, Dad. Three
rocks twirling through the air and landing

perfectly, time after time. He never misses.
The man feels proud. He'd do it all day long

if anyone cared, but even the dog nods off.
Let's say this is some vestigial blip, like that

occasional tail that nurses snip off newborns.
Once his ancestors tossed huge boulders, built

pyramids, even Stonehenge. You wanted
something really big transported? This was

the guy to do it. How many of these leftovers
do we have left? Cave painters shrunk into

tattoo artists, epic poets whose last sparks ignite
greeting-card verse. Just as some day novelists

might morph into the guys who make up menus
for greasy spoons. Today a man flips a stone,

then two more. Presto. See how they join to form
a miniature defiance of the world's natural laws,

a trifling metaphor for the enigmatic? No doubt
about it, the fellow's an artist like any other.

The neighbor's addlepated five-year-old slaps
his head in wonder. At least the first time.

UNEXPECTED HOLIDAY

In the story of Orpheus and Lot's wife
each looks back, but they look at each other:
in such a way do eternal themes get entangled.

Lot's wife, expecting to find the blazing
cities on the plain, sees instead a handsome
young man with a lyre, wearing a lion skin.

Orpheus instead of discovering Eurydice,
his beloved, sees an older woman, the mother
of two grown daughters. Perhaps she is fifty.

Both are surprised. Pardon me, says Orpheus,
I was expecting to meet someone else.
Lot's wife scans the horizon. Where are

Sodom and Gomorrah, she asks, those fun towns?
Neither can answer the question of the other.
Distracted, Orpheus wanders back. Recently,

he says, I've been depressed. Lot's wife sighs:
If you knew how boring it is to share the bed
of a virtuous man. They sit upon warm rocks

beside a rippling stream. Being strangers
to one another, each brings an objective eye
to the other's problems. Perhaps you're

lucky to be free of her, says Lot's wife.
Orpheus makes a similar remark about Lot.
A pious type, he calls him: they always think

they know best. Released from their passions,
they begin to notice the world around them:
the lark's song, light shimmering on clear water.

Orpheus takes comfort in this amiable woman;
Lot's wife is pleased by this polite young man.
Tomorrow perhaps new difficulties will arise,

but not yet. Orpheus leans back against a stone
and begins to sing: nothing too amusing, nothing
too sad: a song about the setting sun reddening

the tamarisk's small clusters of pink flowers
on the first warm evenings in early spring.
It's one of his better songs. Years later new words

will be added about lost love and bloodshed,
the usual themes, but not today. Lot's wife
raises her face to the setting sun and behind

closed lids the world turns pink. Tentatively,
she touches her tongue to her lips to discover
the slightest hint but still distinct flavor of salt.

YELLOW BEAK

A man owns a green parrot with a yellow beak
that he carries on his shoulder each day to work.
He runs a pet shop and the parrot is his trademark.

Each morning the man winds his way from his bus
through the square, four or five blocks. There goes
the parrot, people say. Then at night, he comes back.

The man himself is nondescript—a little overweight,
thinning hair of no color at all. It's like the parrot owns
the man, not the reverse. Then one day the man dies.

He was old. It was bound to happen. At first people
feel mildly upset. The butcher thinks he has forgotten
a customer who owes him money. The baker thinks

he's catching a cold. Soon they get it right—the parrot
is gone. Time seems out of sorts, but sets itself straight
as people forget. Then years later the fellow who ran

the diner wakes from a dream where he saw the parrot
flying along all by itself, flapping by in the morning
and cruising back home at night. Those were the years

of the man's marriage, the start of his family, the years
when the muddle of his life began to work itself out;
and it's as if the parrot were at the root of it all, linking

the days like pearls on a string. Foolish of course, but
do you see how it might happen? We wake at night
and recall an event that seems to define a fixed period

of time, perhaps the memory of a beat-up bike we had
as a kid, or a particular chair where we sat and laughed
with friends; a house, a book, a piece of music, even

a green parrot winding its way through city streets.
And do you see that bubble of air balanced at the tip
of its yellow beak? That's the time in which we lived.

DO THEY HAVE A REASON?

Life begins, you make some friends,
what futures you plan for one another.
No failures here, no one sent to prison.
When you first start out, you can't imagine
you won't succeed, even if the road's unclear,
your parents call you dumb and your brother
pulls your ears; somehow you'll make it work,
even if what you want is to rob a bank,
to be a first-rate crook, but mostly we start out
idealistic—doctors, astrophysicists—or perhaps
we have a taste for fame and money—actors,
stockbrokers—but always something at the top
and always several: Maybe I'll be this or that,
we say. And mostly our friends encourage us
just so we'll encourage them. Sure you'll be
a surgeon, they say, you got the hands. So we
loll about the riverbank with our first cigar
and watch the ducks float by. It's summer
and third grade is dead forever. We lean back
on our elbows and blow some smoke. I'll be
an astronaut, you say, and own a fleet of trucks.
You bet, says your cousin, and I'll play ball.
And he's the guy who dies a drunk at thirty-five.
Think of the moment when you at last catch on.
Some kids get it right away, others not so quick.
One day you experience a click in your head
as the world turns from one place to another.
Does the sky change color, the river get colder?
Like when you stroll into the local diner after school
for a Coke and a hot pretzel, a place you visit
every day to meet your pals, but today your pals
are having fun someplace else and there instead
are half a dozen kids you've never seen before:
sixth graders for certain. They snatch your pack,
toss your stuff around, one tears your shirt,
another rips your books. What's their reason?
They don't need a reason. When the world
you love is changed for another, it's like that.

LIVING IN A NICE PLACE

You enter the whorehouse; tonight it's free.
It could be the boss's birthday, because girls
with big tits puff out the lights, but you hardly

notice as others smooch and take your pants.
In fifty rooms, you'll find fifty ways of having fun.
Why depart, you think, why not stay all week?

Even a year wouldn't be too much, even a lifetime.
Of course, if they were plucking out your toenails,
you'd start to shout, but sweet things like this,

well, what's the harm? Who cares if you don't
read a book or think a worthy thought as long
as your belly's full and prick is spiffy clean?

Truly how terrible is the tyranny of the pleasant.
A prison like any other, but this one tastes sweet:
an endless progression of peaches and cream.

You never consider you might be in danger.
In fact, you're having the time of your life,
although it's hard to say just what you feel.

It's like dying in your sleep—you hop into bed,
flick out the lights, maybe give your limpish prick
a final crank, and a jiffy after that you're gone.

OTHER

Short ones, fat ones, tall ones, thin ones—
Adam had no option when it came to women
and whom to love, no other fish in the sea
or grains of sand for him. Eve was it. And

if she'd had three tits or one black eyebrow,
like a fat caterpillar fixed across her forehead,
that would be the standard by which beauty
must be judged. And Adam too, his small dick,

hairy back and swamp stink were for Eve
merely proof of his perfection; and so they
were stuck not only *with* but *on* each other,
there being no competition. Since then the world

has grown jam-packed with heady choices. Like
a fat man's fork hovering over the over-laden
dessert table at a local diner's All-You-Can-Eat-
For-Ten-Bucks Monday special, years pass

in a state of quivering incertitude as we flit
from one sugar-packed plate to the next,
but are loath to dip for fear of missing an even
sweeter morsel farther on. And once the choice

is made and the couple is leaving the church
each one often thinks, What if I'd waited? What
is Billy or Sally doing now? An idea that nags
at four A.M. after a quarrel or the useless scrutiny

that too many drinks can exact upon the brain.
So that even when seemingly content, the mind
keeps an empty space marked Other, a guest room
with a canopy bed, polar-bear rug and a fireplace

with a small fire always burning, because, surely,
no matter how unlikely, there is still the possibility,
etcetera—a kernel of dissatisfaction that adds a drop
of sadness to an otherwise perfect day. Not so Adam.

Without a nadir, Eve became the acme of perfection.
Nothing else existed until the arrival of the Apple,
since it unleashed the concept of defect and the chance
that something was lacking. Even Time didn't exist,

since without an Other there is scarcely a Next—
next minute, next week—the place where Other
will surely be found. See Adam's hand suspended
an inch from the Apple's sweet pulp. In that instant

Eve's tits begin to sag, the air smells less sweet.
No need even to touch the fruit's hard surface
of false promise—only the hand counts, the extended
digit that directs our steps, signpost of discontent.

THE HAPPILY EVER AFTER

Because the woman thought her husband had talked
too much at their daughter's party, she took his false teeth,
bending over him as if to tell a secret, clasping his jaw
as if in fondness, then snatching out his upper plate.

If he weren't at the end of his third six-pack, he might
have stopped her. But tonight he had come out of his shell,
was describing his time in the war and years in the union,
talking too much, his wife said. Do you see what I've got?

she joked as she raised the teeth above her head, while
the man on the couch looked stricken and pressed his hand
over his mouth, which appeared to have collapsed inward.
Do you have any idea, she asked, how much these cost me?

How do they look? Perhaps there was one nervous laugh
among her daughter's college friends as the woman faked
putting the teeth in her mouth. Oh, Mother, said her daughter,
don't do this—as the mother pirouetted, and she the only one

who hadn't been drinking. The father leaned forward, still
holding his mouth and staring at the floor, too proud to mumble,
too undone to protest. Angry now, the daughter stood up
as her mother danced away, explaining that since the teeth

were brand-new they'd hurt his mouth if he talked too much,
so she'd better tuck them in a safe place. Then she left the room
and decades of little grudges echoed in the clatter of her feet
climbing the stairs. The father lifted his bottle and toasted

his daughter's friends with a scarecrow's smile, feigning
indifference. His shame, the evening's ruin, his wife's cruelty,
the daughter's humiliation—hard to say which was worse,
or so the students thought, ticking off the different dreads.

And one, still single himself, considered the moment
years before when the father was over-swept with the wish
to spend his life with this woman and she pressed him close
and told herself that old story about the happily ever after.

TOWARD SOME BRIGHT MOMENT

Was she drunk? She didn't seem drunk, had only
staggered a little, stumbling over the curb—
a blind woman on the corner of Broadway and Fourth,
kicking her dog, a mutt German shepherd, missing

half the time, and then hitting with a hollow thud,
and shouting, You fuck, and You dumb shit, over
and over. A gray day in March, slush in the streets,
a slight drizzle, a Saturday and the sidewalks packed.

You fuck, yanking the dog and kicking, a woman
in her thirties, her face too twisted with anger
to tell if she was pretty or not; the dog abject
and cringing. No one stopped her, no one said,

You shouldn't do that, and I didn't either, people
giving her a wide berth, perhaps thinking, as I did,
that they couldn't know her pain, that being blind
gave her permission, that her stoicism had at last

collapsed, and wouldn't it collapse for us too,
those of us who could see? But there was the dog
crouched down, attempting to make itself smaller,
with an almost human expression of misery,

but not whining, just waiting for it to be over.
I wanted to cross the street and hit the woman,
knock her down, and I was shocked by this, as if
I'd done something equally wrong; but as she kept

kicking the dog so I wanted to kick her, so angry
did I become, because she didn't stop. In the time
it took me to draw near, slow down, and then pass on,
she kept up her assault, and even with my back turned

I still heard her shouts, while I kept telling myself
how all these other men and women on the street
also saw and heard her. They did as I did. I wasn't alone.
We were all righteous or culpable or comfortable

together. We all passed on, or at least until I had gone,
because I don't know what happened, if she stopped
on her own or if a cop stopped her or someone else
just couldn't bear it anymore. How often this image

comes back to me when I'm depressed or hate myself
or want to be better. I think what I might have done—
rescued the dog, led the woman away—though now
twelve years have passed. Even a certain kind of day

will bring it back, a wet city street, crowds of people
pushing toward some bright moment, the one to make
their lives complete—the wail of a car alarm, a tangle
of yellow cabs, a pigeon in the gutter crushed by a bus.

DEAD ROPE

Chukka, chukka—so he repeats when the waitress
with her butt sheathed in a tight black skirt struts
past his table where he sits with his book—chukka,
chukka—the sound being the imagined chafing

of her thighs or nether cheeks, this being a vestigial
pleasure, now vulgar, caught from his eye's corner,
seventy and winkless, over-the-hill, out to pasture—
chukka, chukka—instead of squeezing those scraps

of fading pleasure from the antique and equally fat,
perhaps over pinochle or park bench, not this chukka,
chukka, not this quick squint, not this wickedness,
sipping his bottom-shelf scotch, faking a book-look,

but not turning the page, not bequeathing the peek
at her perky ass to youth, bad man, because it's a joke,
because scarcely a spark remains to ignite his crotch,
because nothing's down there but dead rope and even

taking a leak is problematic, so why not act his age,
or the age others expect him to act, or do the right
thing and just check out, jump from a cliff, and not
insult all the world with chukka, chukka, the creep?

PENNY FOR YOUR THOUGHTS

J.K. 1938–1999

This is how my friend behaves: first
for two hours he squats on the toilet,
empties himself, empties himself.
Then he takes toilet-bowl cleaner
and scours his thigh till the skin
turns raw. After that with a razor
and without water, he scrapes his face,
dragging the blade along his cheeks,
past his nose, eyes, right to the scalp.
At last he takes his jar of pennies,
and with surgical tape he fastens
a dozen pennies across his forehead,
bends toward the mirror. Is it enough?
This is what you do when your brain's
fucked up and you try to fix yourself
and a tumor is pressed smack against
the frontal bone. You stick pennies there,
you shave it, you scrub away the badness
before you change into a vegetable.
Head scraped and cut, forehead criss-
crossed with tape, spotted with coins
to suck the poison out and his eyes,
I won't tell you about his eyes,
but nearly lost behind the tangle
were the loving eyes I used to know.
It's like one of those jokes. In the good
life you take a little seed and plant it,
then you get a vegetable. In the bad life,
you take the vegetable and plant it.

ALLIGATOR DARK

Stiff as a fireman's spray, his urine smacks
into the toilet bowl to spatter against
the two-inch remnant of a cigarette, either
a Camel or Lucky Strike both of which

his parents smoke. Perhaps he is eight.
A chaste delight in this pre-filter era
before Freudian notions could for him
ruin the simplest of pleasures. The butt's

lipstick reddened tip bleeds into the murk—
Take that, Mom!—till the paper splits apart
and tobacco bits skitter off like peewee
lifeboats. The boy zips his pants as his mother

shouts, What's taking you so long? Just
washing up, he calls back, before flushing
the tiny survivors of the stricken liner down,
down to the alligator dark beneath the streets.

LEARNING TO COPE

Adrift on his back in the tub, the boy detects
the tip of his prepubescent prick as it pokes up
above the surface of the water not unlike
the conning tower of U-boat Number 88
during its mad flight for Buenos Aires after

the German defeat. He, too, the boy thinks,
has known hard times: the bully on the next block,
the ruffians in his third-grade class. The boy
envisions the German captain peering from
the rounded apex of pink nubbin over a sea

upon which a cake of soap bobs between
mountainous knees. Experiencing a moment
of metaphysical delight, the boy asks: Should I
kill them or not? For by now he has packed
the block of Ivory with everyone he likes to hate.

With as much hesitation as a falcon dropping
on a kitten, the boy begins to make exploding
torpedo noises: pop-pop, lipped-closed garglings,
with his spit, as the cake of soap rocks and tiny
screams and final prayers rend the Atlantic air.

Then, his mission done, he drags the washcloth
over the soap like a sheet across a dead man's face.
Out in the hall, the boy's mother hears odd sounds.
Surely, by now the water has grown cold. She too
has her dreams. What future triumphs should

she wish upon her boy? Banker or benefactor,
soldier or senator? How will her young champion
launch himself into the tide of human life?
Temporarily cleansed of his current dislikes,
the boy sits up and the pink tip of his prick

ducks beneath the surface. On to Buenos Aires!—
an escape into the time warp between the fated
and false, a life of good brandy and fat cigars,
where he alone is the only big shot, brass hat
or autocrat fit to say, Stop and Let's cut the shit!

PAYBACK

The hot tip of a spent match accidentally
pokes against the boy's soft scrotum. Ouch!
He had been trying to light his farts, a trick
he has yet to master, and now he is running

out of gas. At first he had twisted around
from the side but couldn't manage the reach,
then he dove down as if touching his toes
to take a swipe from underneath which led

to the sizzling attack on his balls, still hairless
and petit. At last he stretches out on his back
on the bedroom floor. He is naked except for
a Tigers T-shirt and crusty pair of gym socks.

He kicks his legs toward the ceiling, then back
above his head as he directs the flaring match.
In terms of care and concentration, he could be
a rocket engineer as he gropes toward blast off

and transformation into a living flamethrower,
a useful gift when pursued down the block
by the local bully who he now hopes to reduce
to a greasy smudge on the cracked sidewalk.

His little brother's shout disrupts his glad thoughts:
Mom! Junior's being dirty again! Framed between
his upraised legs, the boy sees his mother blossom
in the doorway with an expression of disgust before

the yelling, the snuffed match and hasty yanking
of his body back onto his feet and into his shorts,
actions attended by ever more meager explanations
and his brother's sarcastic remarks. Later, stripped

of his matches and confined to his room, the boy
deconstructs his mother's reproachful look,
the same, he thinks, as she gives their old hound
when he's caught snacking in the cat box, her quick

censure of the dog's surrender to his lower nature;
and though the boy knows he'll be pardoned, his mother's
discovery will form from now on a dark pane of glass,
tinting all her future study of her son. No use detailing

the benefits gained from hurling a fiery discharge
of methane at random pursuers; his mother inhabits
another reality, one less wondrous, where amazing
effects from ho-hum causes are scarce and appear

in black and white. Lessons like these, the boy thinks,
lead one to forgo careers in circuses and seek out
jobs in banks. They pave the ever-constricting path
toward adulthood, while the portrait of upraised ass

and flaming match will possess in family memory
the permanence of a framed Picasso above the mantel.
Such are time's hard truths softened only by the soon
to be savored delight of beating his brother to a pulp.

THE BALANCE

Red-eyed men and harridans—Cain and his brood
trudge across the desert waste, lugging a pallet
with Cain's wife and brats perched on heaps
of fetid pelts. You know it's hot and they missed

lunch—rocks and yellow dirt, no water in sight,
nobody smiling, nobody standing up straight—
a twenty-foot painting in the Musée d'Orsay.
Who knows how Cain acquired such a family,

one of those lacunae in the Book of Genesis
that kids worry about—if Adam and Eve had
only three sons, and Cain had several wives,
where did he get them? It's a big imponderable.

But in the evening when the clan has stopped
to make camp and family members are snacking
on lizards, slow raw rabbit, if lucky a prickly
pear, and what can be dug from beneath rocks,

then Cain sits under a cactus, ponders the fiery
glow to the west and has philosophical thoughts.
What is beauty to this man, what brings delight?
Does he pick up a sharp stone and think, Nice

shape, I could smash a person's head with this?
Does he admire the color of a squashed newt?
I prefer to believe he has no regrets. What's done
is done and Abel is less than a hyena's lunch.

In the d'Orsay I saw no postcards of this painting,
didn't recognize the name of the artist—a work
most likely exhibited because of its peculiarity—
Cain's thorny journey occupying all of one wall.

Normally, it's Abel who receives our respect:
a nice guy who tended his sheep, well-spoken

and mild, struck down by his brother for giving
his first lamb to god. But it's Cain and his bunch

who I can't forget, nomads with bent backs, not
known for their jokes, mostly greedy, no strangers
to jealousy and envy, quick to anger, but needed
to acknowledge my divided self. I like to think

I have a little window in my chest—there's Abel
well-washed in a white shirt and reading good books;
there too is Cain in a stinking lion skin, sharpening
a rock in his shack fixed to the left side of my heart.

FAMILY VALUES

Cocksman par excellence, or so the Koran
would have us think—Adam fathering forty
thousand kids in his nine hundred and thirty years.

Eve being knocked up was a version of stuttering,
or like the hiccoughs, since for scarcely a second
was she ever unpregnant, while after the first fifty

one shake of the leg sufficed to send her progeny
skipping across the floor of their hut. And missed
shots and miscarriages, Adam had to be always

checking his trajectory and priming his weapon. Such
is our pedigree and today when the President speaks
of family values these are the folks he has in mind—

pinups for the Creationists and Anti-Rubber League.
Shame on me for wasting my time scribbling jokes
when I could be out sowing the fields with my seed.

But who at Adam's house did the dishes with another
four brats born each year, who scrubbed the loin-
cloths and made the beds when each day a hundred kids

demanded birthday presents? Had Adam desired
to be a poet, where could he find the quiet? As for Eve,
forget it, she churned out enough milk to float an ark.

Adam's only job was to give his prick a set of legs
so when he wasn't pursuing god's work by fucking
his brains out, he was most likely soaking his organ

in an icy stream. Did he call it Sir and give his forelock
a deferential tug as he did with the almighty? When
the President talks of fighting for freedom, he means

this: the fuss of bashing a current crop of bad guys upsets
his focus on constant sex with beer and beer steaks in
between, because how could Adam explore the niceties

of original sin when he hardly had the opportunity
to take a breather? His prick cracked the whip, though
whenever he had the chance he snuck off to hammer

on the Garden's gates, eager to escape to a spot
he recalled as pre-sex. Yes, like a squirrel smushed
between two Mack trucks, Adam was stuck between

two autocrats, as the almighty flung down thunderbolts
to force him back to the sack to breed more brats
and angels dive-bombed his head like ferocious jays.

(2004)

HIDE AND SEEK

At first it's just a form of play. Your mother
shuts your eyes or hides them with her hand.
For a moment, she is gone. Are you afraid? Then,

surprise, she's back again. A few years later,
your favorite game is hide and seek. You wait
behind a tree as your best friend counts to ten.

Then, when it's your turn, you search for him.
Doesn't this suggest the impossibility
of getting lost? Your mother uncovers your eyes,

your friend uncovers your hiding place—
the world's machinery won't let you disappear.
As you grow older you read of runaways returned,

stolen children found again. We long to believe
the world wants each of us in our own spot,
safe and respected, even the unfortunate held dear.

Yet increasingly on the street you see the lost,
men and women adrift between destinations.
Do you see that man in the park behind the tree?

He waits for someone to finish counting.
Then you notice a man on a bench, a woman
idly smoking. Don't they, too, seem to be waiting?

If the first part of your life attempts to prove
you can't be lost, what belief directs the rest,
or are you lost from the start? That man watching

from the bench, do you see how he listens?
Does he think someone seeks him even now?
Does he regret he concealed himself so well?

You look from the window of a passing bus,
but as the man stands up, he sees you go by,
glances back as if at a scrap of paper the wind

flicks down the street. Briefly, you feel alarm.
Lost, lost, you ask, when were we ever found?
Now it begins to rain. The man slips from sight

as the bus turns and stops, starts and turns again.
You forget but don't quite forget as you watch
people with pursuits much like your own hurry

between two points—not quite lost, not yet found.
Consider this: our first breath brought us here
and as sparks rise up from a fire so we disappear.

SURVIVOR

Carrots snitched from a neighbor's garden, coated
with dirt that no amount of rubbing on my pants
or sleeve could quite scrape off, the mix of sweetness

and grit against my teeth, I feel it even yet—
four years old, the war going on—I called it
living off the land. The war was elsewhere, death

occurring at great distance, or so it seemed
from adult talk, just as the twenty-mile trip
from Chatham to New York seemed a great distance.

Along that road a diner, knocked together
from the gutted body of a plane, pointed
one wing at the street, and it made sense to think

it had been shot down a year or two before,
just as it made sense in Penn Station to see
soldiers on crutches or otherwise bandaged.

The day another plane, its motor roaring,
plummeted toward our house, it made sense to think
it had to crash; and I hid behind the trash cans,

waiting for the explosion. Or the day a chunk
of plaster as big as a coffin lid fell
from the kitchen ceiling and I had to be told

it wasn't the war; even the day the neighbor
next door slaughtered his chickens with a hatchet
and a dozen birds scattered headless across

the grass. Given what I knew about the world
it made perfect sense—the posthumous squawking,
thin whips of blood spouting from their neck stumps.

REPARATIONS

Slowly you work to raise the gates of your life.
So much time has gone by. The chains are rusty.
The rasp of the links dragged across the pulleys
makes a cry almost like you might make yourself.

From within, you hear the quarreling of brutes,
the snapping and click of teeth as the creatures
get themselves ready. Hurry, warn the villagers
whose cottages lie in the valley. But it's too late.

The iron gates reach the top, shudder and stop.
Cautiously, you look inside. Is no one around?
Dead leaves skitter across the paving stones.
Where are the beasts you wouldn't let escape?

Then, by the wall, you see a child gnawing a bone.
The fury of his blue eyes strikes you like a blow.

BETWEEN

His life's circus tent trembles on its central pole,
torn canvas, faded stripes, while across the alley,
the circus tent of his dream rears up indestructible—
between runs a rat heaven bright with broken glass.

Within the tent of his life, his wife and son complain;
the wife wants better, the son wants more, a dog farts.
An old Chevy flecked with rust is propped on blocks;
shelves of unread books, trunks of half-baked plans.

Within his tent of dream, his mistress struts in black boots
and cracks a whip—her golden tits the only source of light.
His own best sellers pack the shelves. His son's a priest,
his wife is at the beach, a red Ferrari obscenely pouts.

And the man himself, where are his own days spent?
Unable to pick one place or discard either, he has chosen
rat heaven, hurrying across the broken glass from one tent
to the other, peering into each, finding a home in neither.

FACE-TO-FACE

That line between where I stop and the world
starts has been vague of late and I can't take
a step without bumping against that layering

of barbed wire and brick which is my grand
exclusion. Once it was porous, or so it seemed,
scarcely more than a suburb of myself where

glad hands beckoned and vistas of billboards
bragged of the delights of advancement. That
has since stopped. In its place stands a frontier

like one between some third-world country
and the great, where border guards grill me
on my plans. Do I mean to set off bombs

or rape the young? I sit on a hardwood bench
as they check my papers, while out the window
to the other side songbirds twitter symphonies.

Soon sent packing back to where I came from,
I linger near the gate, waiting for the shift change
so I can confront these fellows face-to-face.

But wouldn't they go home the other way?
you ask. Quite the reverse, these men work for me
and return to houses I have built. The food

they eat, the clothes they wear, their very dreams
are mine. But no matter. Freed at last from their
daily labor, they hurry past without a word.

AT HOME WITH ANGELS

A man was fed up, at the end of his tether,
but he was a good shot and knew what
he was after. Yet not from a duck blind,
or tree stump; his own porch and 12-gauge

were good enough to pop one, then another
out of the sky. As for the angels, a glitch
in their fixed routine had by ill fortune
directed their flight path over his rooftop,

flitting from one dimension to the next,
back and forth each day on missions
of rescue or retribution. One might think
the man didn't understand the true nature

of his offense, but no, he knew full well
their celestial origin, but his life was packed
with quarrel and complaint, and the plans
he had made, he saw how they lay strewn

like spilled coins. He even knew the value
of the angels' mission, the goodly enterprise
of Heaven. Yet it meant nothing when set against
all that rankled. Only at home did he find peace

when he beheld the noble heads and lofty wings
mounted in rows upon his wall. Once again
their halos beckoned as the angels, in fancy only,
rushed toward his personal salvation. Nothing

he believed, of course, but briefly he gave in
to what he called his weakness as he permitted
the illusion of love and compassion to enliven
the frozen chambers of his ordinary heart.

THE PERSONAL LYRIC VS. THE PUBLIC GOOD

It wasn't simply sex that Samson longed for,
or not quite, but to lay down the lord's burden.
Tough to be a soldier each day, slaughtering
the infidel for an invisible general when your

passion is to sneak off after battle to scribble
lyrics of personal celebration or complaint.
So when Delilah appeared with her tangle
of black hair, nearly bursting from her garment,

and said, Peel me a grape, Samson forgot
about slaughter and fell victim to his creative
nature. As for the lord and his chosen people
they couldn't compete with an art personified

by such a heroic physique. Samson climbed her
as a fireman climbs a ladder, until exhausted
he collapsed into sleep. Then, as he napped,
his magic hair was cut and eyes plucked out.

Perhaps the world has had worse awakenings—
Mrs. Lot turned to a block of salt, Adam
driven from the Garden—but for Samson
Delilah's voluptuous distraction was forgotten,

and he was over-swept by his own dark thoughts—
those internal whines of what-might-have-beens
that pass for philosophy. Of course once his hair
grew back, Samson was granted a second chance.

Dragged out to the Philistines' crowded temple
he brought the place tumbling down, thus packing
his enemies off to their reward; and Delilah, too,
that pretty body, dispatched to whatever heaven

her people possessed, since she had done her best,
was a heroine of sorts. So think of Delilah as the artist
and Samson the hack, because as he had dashed off
his private lyrics, applauding her every pubic hair

and tootling the imperfections of his soul, Delilah
had devoted her work to the larger good, and by giving
her body to that bloodstained bully, she had written epics,
carved public statues, played Samson like a symphony.

COMMOTION

Tom asked, Are those sharks? and I looked.
We were teetering warily along a narrow strip
of planks laid in a long arc on top of the water.

With each step the planks sunk a bit beneath
the surface but still seemed firm, vanishing
in front and behind, spanning the bay. It was

almost sunset after a day of unsettled weather.
Ahead through a split in thick clouds the sun
hung a few inches over the water, pouring forth

its red and golden radiance. My feet were wet
but I felt calm as I scanned the horizon for sharks.
Most nights my dreams are all work, a ditch

I keep digging in my sleep, but this one came
as a gift, for far to the south I saw a commotion
in the water—row after row of some creature,

plunging ahead, rising and sinking, like horses,
but not horses, with ears flapping behind them
and their muzzles raised. The day's last light

shone on their wet fur—brindle or tan, black
or spotted with white—hundreds, stretching off
in the distance, a furious energy of forward motion

as their paws broke the surface and they arced
through the white froth. They had nothing to do
with us, but would cross our path a short way

farther on. Tom and I had paused in our careful
progression. No, I said, they're not sharks. They're
Great Danes. Oh, said my friend, I was wondering.

For Thomas Lux

SCOFFLAW

That woman walking toward you down the street—
straight back, head erect—sometimes it seems
you construct her step by step. By you, I mean
the men, or the lion's share at least; as for the ladies,

you may turn the page, these matters don't call for
your attention. But you men, at first you might notice
her breasts pressing against her white silk blouse,
as heavy as the heads of infants, then her thin waist,

her thighs stroking the trim lines of her skirt, neither
long nor short, dark and of some clinging fabric,
then comes the descent down, down to the golden
ankle chain, scarlet toenails, where you reverse

yourself like reclimbing a long flight of stairs,
often pausing for breath at each revisited locality
as its mix of intimacy and recollection gives over
a renewed pleasure. Only now do you see her face—

framed by shoulder-length hair swaying with each
step; chin, full lips—your glance spiraling inward
till you reach her eyes. This construction—it's like
a house that arrives on the back of a flatbed truck

for you to hammer together. At first, as you impose
your deliberation upon her, you think of little more
than leading her to some spot by a mountain brook
and slowly unbuttoning her blouse—nothing special,

no lovecuffs or leather—but by the time you reach
her eyes' blue intimacy you have passed to discourse—
pot roast, politics, the subject has no importance—
until when the whole woman has been assembled,

a benign future begins to unfold itself—summer
on the shore, winter weekends on the slopes—clichés
so stultifying that you can hardly stand to admit them
even to yourself. Then she's gone and perhaps three

seconds have elapsed. What you have constructed,
this fiction from seduction to banality, is soon forgotten.
The street snaps back to life. Dogs bark; a car honks.
You readjust your step to allow for the sidewalk's

unexpected elasticity. Perhaps you are hurrying
to the dentist or to buy a quart of milk, even to pay
that traffic ticket because you too, in small ways,
break the law. Okay, ladies, you can come back now.

HACK WORK

My private Baghdad began when the furnace broke down
in the dead of winter. Plumber, painter, heating contractor—
where I saw wreckage, they saw opportunity.

It was after Christmas and temperatures crashed.
The house was closed up and the water pipes burst.
My private Baghdad began when the furnace broke down.

The bathroom and parlor flooded, ruining the rug.
It was my very own oil crisis; I called whomever I could.
Where I saw wreckage, they saw opportunity.

Nobody was killed, but the toilet tank shattered;
no bombs fell, but the bathroom ceiling collapsed.
My private Baghdad began when the furnace broke down.

Although bigger, Saddam Hussein's living room on TV
looks no worse than mine. Marines recline on broken divans.
Where I see wreckage, they find opportunity.

There's always money to be made. Just whose freedom
matters most? White panel trucks pack the driveway.
My private Baghdad began when the furnace broke down;
where I saw wreckage, others found opportunity.

DANCE, DANCE

They have become quite a crowd: the ones
who have passed over, grouping to one side
like pieces lost in a game of chess. Wrongly,

you think of them as indifferent; rather,
they have grown more judgmental than ever.
But not with malice. Everything personal

has been stripped from them and their vision
has become exact. Or such is your concern.
Let's say you cheat at cards, cheat at work,

cheat on a spouse—how does this affect
the thoughts of those to whom your thoughts
are now open? The friend dead of a heart attack

on a city street—how does he see your actions
now that he has moved to the side of inaction?
If there is a question, it's one of scale. In death,

they keep growing, until they dwarf the board
on which they played, while that steady shrinkage
of a final pawn, is that what lies ahead? Better

work harder, that's one option. Or perhaps blot
the whole mix from your mind with distraction.
Whatever you select, it won't stop their meddling,

or what you regard as meddling, in your life.
See how they multiply, while your presence
contracts as the light fades. Now their ranks

press together as they rise above you. Is it time
for a capitulation? But you won't join them yet.
You have vital work to fill your waking hours,

although it is nothing they would call worthy.
Dance, dance—the dead form the wall against which
your shadow plays in the light cast up by the world.

SHARDS OF BROKEN GLASS REJOINED

9/11/01

My dear, do you recall the day we stood
in that museum room while on four walls
around us hung Monet's four great paintings
of water lilies, with their dozens of variations
of green, the quick strokes of light, until the lilies
seemed to stir on the water's surface and the walls
were transformed, canvas vanished, water breathed
as the blossoms in their emerald wreaths drifted
on the multicolored calm? Although the room
was full, I remember no one else, neither you
nor our daughter, as I turned and the pond circled
around me as though I stood still. Had I a religion
it would be this, so small did I feel, so great
a gladness and self-forgetting overtook me,
as if all the world had been brought into that room,
hung on those walls: the pond with the willows
rising above it, green of all green, flowers like
all the disunited repatched and mended, light
like shards of broken glass rejoined.
                                        I must
think of this today when I keep seeing a sky
filled with paper, a floating curtain of scraps,
some burnt or scorched or still ablaze against
that larger flame and the sky's mockery of blue.
It was as if that paper included Monet's canvases
reduced to torn smidgens, inconsequential specks
floating over the city, because doesn't it all
seem so much smaller, as if suddenly a color
had appeared so bright to turn the others gray,
a noise so loud to change all talk to a whisper,
as if skulls floated on the surface of the water?
What a task now lies ahead, to search the streets,
bent like crooked hoops. Here lies a canvas leaf,
a portion of a flower, a twig, a bud, a bit of sun.

Does this swirl of blue fit this flicker of green
or this scrap of light go on top? Let others seek
an answer among the world's varieties of murder.
We have our own sanity to reconstruct.

SAYING NO

He stretches out his right hand,
then pulls it back with the left.
His lips part to fashion a kiss,
irony shoves itself into the space.
At one moment he dismantles a wall,
the next he builds it up again.
What does he fear? He imagines being
shrunk down to a pool of salt water.

The child he once might have been
sits on the bank with his fishing pole.
Blind fish nose violently past his hook.
They could take it, let the barb sink deep
into lip or cheek. They choose not.

Even discontent is better than nothing.
Even a denial can be an affirmation.

NO MOMENT PAST THIS ONE

I tell you, it seems always to be out there.
Is it like a blanket? No, it is nothing
like a blanket. Is it like darkness?
No, neither is it like darkness. But it
doesn't act like something inside me.
How do I know this? Because it seems
to be waiting. And it seems to have both
hunger and humor. And it seems both
patient and eager, ponderous and weightless.
And it is large. And it grows larger. How
can it not be like darkness when it devours
the light? How can it not be like a blanket
when it seems so all-enveloping? How
can it seem like a place to tumble into
and still be so tireless, so agile? Yet if I
could answer such riddles, then perhaps,
perhaps, but when it comes it wraps me
in soft ropes, and it draws the life from me
and yet I continue to breathe, even though
there seems no moment past this one
and this one, and the days continue to pass.
You see, it must come from someplace outside,
some cold place or from deep in the earth,
because if the beast dwelt within me, then
how could I live, how could it be withstood?

For Liz Rosenthal

ODDS AND ENDS

Beneath a pile of papers, bills, accumulated
odds and ends, lay that snapshot of the cove
where your wife threw your ashes, a picture
happened upon once again while searching

for something else—phone number, tax bill—
now for the time being forgotten. She had
shown me the place and I lifted my camera:
simple enough—a hazy autumn afternoon

on the Mediterranean about fifty miles north
of Barcelona three years ago. Now I lean over
the dining-room table: a U-shaped cove with
the surf frosting the line between green water

and pebbly beach. On the far side a gable-shaped
sprawl of black rocks rises against a mass of trees.
A man looks toward us from that distant corner
of green water, rocks and sand, too far away

to guess more than his sex. What was it like
for your wife to walk toward the water's edge
with the small box of you? Already at thirty-five
she had lost her parents, all her other relatives.

It made it easier to grieve, she said, I had done it
so often. So she must have been businesslike,
knowing the form, no matter how difficult
the feeling. I threw them, she explained. Ash

and bone—scattered across the water's surface,
then not waiting to watch you drift away at this
favorite spot where you both had frequently swum.
That man on the far side of the cove, I wanted

to think he might be you, looking in this direction
one last time. This morning I had my plans,
bills to pay, the necessary errands that fill a life.
What a mess of papers lay scattered on the table.

So one by one I sorted through them for a bill
or a phone number, I no longer recall, and there
I saw your cove of green water, this remnant
of that hazy day when I walked with your wife.

Here is the place I threw his ashes, she said,
I *threw* them, then turned my back, hurried away.
And I drew out my camera to hide my emotion—
the black rocks, the hissing surf on the shale.

Across the cove, a man watched us. I thought,
that man over there, why can't he be you?
A day in late autumn, a haze in the air—
I snapped my picture; we walked back to the car.

THE BIRTH OF ANGELS

The heavy-lidded enterprise of the dead
begins with forgetting, ends with forgotten.
Like smoke, so thick at first but higher
just a wisp, until it is indistinguishable

from air. The move from youth to old age,
doesn't it resemble falling, a leaf descending
from white birch to front lawn? You think
it drifts slowly? It plummets. And this well-

dressed elderly man crossing against the light.
At the curb he puts a hand to his chest. He feels
a fluttering which suggests the birth of angels:
a sudden consciousness, the thrashing of wings.

JONAH'S FLIGHT TO TARSHISH

His mail, mostly bills, was already being forwarded,
and each day his new landlady expected his arrival.
To welcome him, she had painted the spare room,
bought a bed and dresser, nothing exceptional—
a comfortable chair because, from what she heard,

he liked to read. As a widow with grown children
she looked forward to this respectable gentleman
with settled habits who might help about the house,
hammer the random nail, even carry the groceries,
and was it wrong to hope for a greater intimacy,

a companion to share her long evenings? Going out
each morning to sweep the walk, she'd gaze past
her gate toward the sea. Oh, the waves, the waves—
how they rush forward and retreat as if they've just
heard a story, which they have chosen not to repeat.

FUNCTIONAL FORGETTING

Here is the world, here the world's forgetting:
the left and right hand tugging at one another.
As he runs his tongue up the inside of her thigh,
the world retreats. But that was yesterday.

At first just the touch of her hand would send
the world spinning into darkness. Then it took
a kiss, then the exposing of a breast. How
these confessions age us. Is this why the old

become forgetful? Death's envoy must be Wonder.
Once again a touch becomes electric. As we stagger
toward our ultimate minute, the world grows rich
with opportunity. Ah, Death, unloose your thighs.

THE APPRECIATION OF BEAUTY

Prime Mover took a breather to admire the view:
sunrise in the valley made green grass glitter.
Belly full of breakfast, Prime Mover expressed wind:
hot gases, minuscule particles rushed outward.

Tell me, is a day equally long for fruit fly
and tiger? Within one universe, can't a cluster
of atoms enclose another? Amidst swirling methane
at least one particle contained a flicker of life.

Jiffies in one world, millenniums in another.
The presence of water, the presence of light:
soon fire was discovered, then the wheel.
Prime Mover sighed, rubbed his belly, strolled on.

Science and religion intertwined when on one speck
a white-coated upstart hypothesized the Big Bang.

ENDNOTES FROM THE ANCIENT WORLD

With their liver-spotted hands gripping their crotches,
these old men, sitting on benches across the street
from the Leaning Tower of Pisa, know what it's like
not to get it up. Despite its beauty of form, the intricate

design of white stone, it leans and each year declines
a little more. The old men sigh. The world bullies us
with metaphor. Rome is packed with busted columns
and oldsters creeping home. Each year Venice sinks

a little deeper into the muck, and they too. It's wrong
to think that history's lessons are confined to books
when every rusty car retells a sorry story. Old men gather
in the marketplace to pinch the fruit, but are themselves

shortchanged. A few surround a statue of the goddess
Venus. Though busted up and missing limbs, her tits
are as perky as ever. One old guy reaches out to touch
her thigh, warmed by the afternoon sun, and in his brain

he hears a sudden humming as he recalls a girl's perfume,
a summer night, all the never-to-be-repeated clichés. Then
it's gone. This is the way the road runs and while the men
may not complain, it came as a surprise. Does it dignify

their plight to be mocked by art? Like butchered centaurs
on a Grecian urn, perhaps they find relief in the joint nature
of their defeat. Defining the defining male act at ninety,
the comic quipped, It's like shooting pool with a rope.

THE PIG'S COMPLAINT TO HIS QUEEN

Circe drove the men into her pens,
and they assumed the shape of pigs . . .
but their minds stayed the same as before.
                                              —Odyssey
                                    after Drummond de Andrade

Dear Mistress, ponder the frailty of human flesh.
What amplitude can the idea of the sphere provide
for those formerly elongated and lacking in bulk?
No roundness or pinkness dignifies their thought.

They lack the nobility that attends colossal girth
and seek release from God's greatest gift: the snout.
Why have you set these brutish sailors among us?
They scorn the savory acorn and mock the tender

morsels it is our delight to take from beneath rocks.
They derive no comfort from the conciliatory mud.
Despite the subtle flexing of their supple ears,
they are unable to orchestrate the evening zephyrs.

Reflect upon the ashen ugliness of the human foot,
a reptilian form culminating in a fringe of flesh:
the toes. You would think they would be grateful
to obtain the sturdy virtues of the cloven hoof,

with its reverse heart shape, acme of porcine beauty,
and the upward slant of its ebony configuration
creating the delicate tiptoe step that compares
so favorably to the dance. Yet they do not frolic.

The grunts they make to the moon they call singing.
The scratches they make in the dirt they call art.
Cheerless, they introduce our piglets to the vice
of melancholy as they stare into the restless waves

or the dust of the curving road that knows no end.
Yet no destination can grant them gratification,
no particular moment can give them joy. They seek
not being but constant becoming, not this moment

but the next. At night their needlelike laments
to their lanky gods puncture the rotundity of sleep
and deflate our dreams, leaving us fitful and alert,
unable to recover the former comfort of our sties.

CHUCKLEHEADS

Philistines, the chuckleheads, I've known a couple—
they wipe their clumsy feet on poetry's bright carpet,
they add their whistling to the notes of the quartet.
At times they're called critics; they like making trouble.

But the first Philistines, good or bad, who can say?
Foes to the Jews, sure, but they must have had qualities.
They weren't circumcised, but loved their kids. Donkeys
and oxen were their beasts of burden, working all day

till they keeled over, left to rot by the side of the road—
like the jawbone of an ass that Samson used to clobber
a thousand Philistines to bits, a beast that worked hard,

was meek of heart and got paid in beatings for its labor,
had already slipped from memory's pocket when Samson
seized its jaw to whop those chuckleheads, the Philistines.

HEAVEN'S PROLETARIAT

Like pimples, baby teeth or the chance
of testicular cancer, as a man grows older
so his soul gets squeezed out, no longer able
to lounge about in commodious accommodations.

It would seem that as a person gets larger
there would be more space, but that's not
the case. Casualty to puberty, delighting
in his appetites, the man gets so jam-packed

with contradictory inclinations that his soul
is lucky just to cling tightly to his belt, perch
on a shoulder, and would be ejected altogether
if the man didn't need it for convincing coloration

when applying for a loan at the bank or telling
a cutie on their first date, Of course I respect you.
Like breaking up rocks or digging a ditch,
it's thankless work for Heaven's proletariat;

and in time a bent back, black eyes and bruises
reduce their psalm-singing to discordant *J'accuse*s.
In fact, the richer and more successful becomes
the soul's assigned host, the more the soul aches.

Often at night a dozen meet to discuss their fate.
My gentleman just won big at the track. Oh, no!
My lady's lover just gave her a mink coat. Oh, no!
Then one soul creeps home to his master, squats

on the fellow's pillow ready to pack his dreams
with complaint, but how peacefully he sleeps,
so that his very silence seems to suggest a yet
unseen proof of decency. Ah, despite the bad times,

he loves him and planting a kiss on his cheek the soul
retreats to his spot on the wall. The man jerks awake
from a sudden pain. A moonbeam lights up an insect,
settling into the ceiling's darkest corner, perhaps a spider.

The man knows the world is full of the poor, the dirty
and the dumb that serve no function—and now this bug
has come to befoul his room. Too lazy for pursuit, he slips
back toward sleep, meaning to squash it in the morning—

see him as a citizen with a normal number of failings
and sporadic virtues, whose soul now shrinks a trifle more
into a bit of ash, a mote in the eye, a single black spot
too trifling to trouble any sinner's untroubled sight.

ANGEL WITH BOOK

Bear with me on this—the man at the urinal
was reading a book. His fly was unzipped
and the choked tip of his prick poked above
the elastic strip of his white Jockey shorts—
a man about sixty at a turnpike rest stop.

I came, I peed, I watched, I went, although
I dawdled a little as the fellow flipped a page
or two, gripping the book with both fists
as his prick's tip turned blue—an Agatha
Christie mystery. Who knows how late

he stayed after I left. A minute? But I like
to think he reached the end before gangrene
set in. The next week I stopped by again
and the man was gone, although perhaps
he had been rushed away in an ambulance

just seconds before. On both days I was racing
between Boston and New York with one eye
on the clock and the other checking for cops,
while this man had found a spot to be happy in.
But I didn't see it then for my grasp of the dark

needed a serious boost before I came to think
it unimportant what he read. Still, as I returned
to the automotive brawl, I was sure I'd seen
one of life's mysteries. What depths did I reach
before I understood that an angel with a green

down parka and cheap book had shown up
to give me a sign? Only the routine defeats
and setbacks fixed in any stumbler's path,
but not so much the failures as the attendant
rush, living life like topping off a grocery list

at full speed with a busted three-wheeled cart
through some Super-Jumbo's constricted and
dimly lit aisles, packed with the halt, the lame

and mentally thick, which made me see at last
that the fellow at the rest stop had got it right:

that the book and choked prick didn't count,
the meaning of the act offset the substance,
that is, the value of self-forgetting and total
obliteration of the quotidian. Who cares about
the rest compared to that? Well, sad to say,

I still did, but at least I'd gotten a first-rate map
for the day I hit the road again. So, angel or not,
when this guy's prick starts to rot, he gets my vote
for a purple heart, even a medal of honor for his act
of valor: a soldier facing battle on life's front line.

THE REQUISITE GRIN

You'd shove her up against a wall and fuck her,
just like I would, if you got the chance, the young
lesbian tells me, speaking of a popular singer

better known for her strategically arranged
bits of clothing than her voice. It's not a name
I recognize, though I know the type. However,

I try to imagine the basic act: to trick, trap
or toss the singer smack against the brick
and strip away the scraps of designer cloth.

Presumably she would resist, protest, scream
bloody murder. Am I excited by the thought?
I'm afraid I'd mind the bother, I tell my friend,

as I consider how the neighbors would react.
What's more, the singer would think ill of me.
The woman eyes me doubtfully. Your dreams

sure aren't mine, she answers. What are mine?
I wonder. The stripped singer sprawled on a mat
like pink meat offers the sexual moment only;

what cure is that for solitude, the self even yet
condemned to the precincts of self? I think
of the lack of talk, not gossip, but conversation,

the meat abandoned as simply meat, no person
arising from this most intimate act, the fuck
being beginning, middle and end of the flight

from isolation. My young friend waits as I start
to deflect her words with a joke, also a retreat
from talk, interchange of self with self. Better

a full meal than the snack your singer would offer,
I say. My friend grins the requisite grin. We return
to the impersonal. Soon we could be anyone.

OLD FARTS' BALL

Crick, crack, my aching back, takes the place
of the music we lack. The music we hear
rings not in the ear, but rises up from within
our interior. The people we knew
forty years ago have new faces now;
the old don't show. A voice may come through,
a trick of the eye, but we're all in disguise—
is it me, is it you? And the ballrooms
we danced in, do we dance in them yet?
My feet feel so heavy, my fingers don't snap.
His prick's just a memory, her tits bump
her knees, my prick's three floors above us
watching sports on TV. The years in between—
some good, some bad—not lost, say not lost,
just briefly unseen. We keep them nearby,
of that we are sure, and pat purses and pockets
for what we hold dear, not just snapshots
of grandkids, families galore, but a fat
deck of cards—Christ, what a bore. But I'll
look at yours if you look at mine, our jobs,
homes and names, the groups we have joined.
We mull over the missing, the dead
and indifferent, the sick or the working,
whoever is absent. We go over the names,
still someone is lacking. Why, it's yourself
you've mislaid, who you yet hope to find here,
the late adolescent you barely remember.
Have you looked in the bathroom, the lobby
or bar? Have you looked out the window
where the night presses close, where the trees
in the rainstorm gesture and bow? If you saw him
you'd know him, of that you are sure. We turn
toward the glass—there we are, there we are,
a dark line of figures at the edge of the lawn.
What do they think of us, after all this time,
the roads we have taken, the goals met or lost?
What do they think of us? Don't even ask.

Shimer College reunion, 2003

THE MERCY OF LAZARUS

Groggy, sure, and in the midst of bad dreams,
it must have been a dispirited awakening—
expecting everything settled, the long night
without interruption suddenly interrupted,

like a four A.M. alarm bell but worse, the rock
rolled back, to be called forth, told to pick up
the yoke, to pay your bills, get the roof fixed,
to become a bit of proof in the lord's affidavit.

Now the crowd pushes forward, demanding
to hear your cries of thanks. If you refused,
crawled back to your tomb, well, their hope,

lately upraised, would need a tomb of its own.
Where would be His miracle without your deceit—
your laugh and eager shout, the outstretched arms?

DRIVING PAST TOWARD THE BRIDGE

Radiant autumn morning sunlight heats
the broken sidewalk of the Nyack crack house,
where a young black woman in a green wrap

and of questionable reputation scoops glops
of cat food onto a torn page of the day's paper.
A piebald kitten waits, its legs as stiff and gangly

as a new colt's. Busted front steps, chipped siding—
sheets of opaque plastic are tacked across windows
from which at night there's just a glimmer of light

as men from the street corner trail back and forth
and women loiter. Who knows what goes on inside?
Nothing nice. But this morning the sky sparkles;

the weather has changed to warm as the woman
grips the top of her wrap and taps the open can
on the paper while the cat quivers in anticipation.

The young woman's face is as round as the moon—
a parenthetical instant that could pass for joy,
as ripples of heat skitter over the cracked concrete

and dead leaves pirouette. The kitten snatches a few bites,
then wrestles the scrap of paper off the curb to crawl
beneath a parked truck, its greasy and protective dark.

THE SIDEBOARD'S MAHOGANY SURFACE

Snip, snap, the man flicks out the downstairs lights,
then climbs the stairs to bed. The dog's been walked,
his children sleep, his wife unpins her hair. Perhaps
he'll read his book or devote ten minutes to love.

The house sighs. This is when the day's unfinished
sentences, forgotten intentions, set-aside actions,
all the first thoughts that second thoughts erased,
complete their arcs to reach imagined conclusions.

Say you were rushing upstairs to find your alabaster
elephant, but forgot and brushed your teeth instead.
This is the hour when the elephant, left hanging
all day, is at last reclaimed and thus allowed to rest.

But those arguments begun and harsh words bit back—
like you have never known anyone half so stupid—
or the fourth drink you decided not to take, the girl
with big tits who you had almost resolved to call;

or how you had nearly determined to quit your job
and do no more than fish for trout—all these snippets
still hover in the air. And your wife's thoughts too—
maybe the man next door is looking pretty good—

and your kids' assorted incompletions, even the dog's
decision not to bite the mailman, at least for today.
All night these truncated unfinishments swirl and lurch
toward hypothetical closure—trout caught, tit groped,

the mailman bit. How else could tomorrow ever begin?
How else could there be room for all the new false starts
and quick reversals? By dawn the air has begun to settle,
some compromise between the *Is* and *If* and *Almost*

has been reached and at first light the golden particles
filter down and come to rest. An alarm clock rings,
the day begins. Soon a friend arrives. Today's her day
to drive the kids to school. Out of bad habit, she draws

a finger across a sideboard's mahogany surface to reveal
a telltale trail. On her raised fingertip sunlight sparkles
on the minuscule scraps of yesterday's might-have-beens.
The woman frowns, begins to speak, then bites her tongue.

THE SACRIFICE

At the fifteenth floor of a high-class high-rise,
a man in love creeps along a narrow ledge
between his apartment and the next to catch
his girlfriend doing what he thinks she ought not.

The jealousy that, like a dagger piercing his gut,
touched off his initial foolhardy step has shrunk
by now to terror, while visions of Agnes wrapped
in the grip of José, her health club's physical trainer,

begin to grow dim. At first he had pictured the lout
stuck to her naked body like a barnacle to a rock,
but with each sidewise lurch along the windblown lip
a reordering of priorities takes place, till at midpoint

above six lanes of traffic he shouts out the words
of the old song to the world at large, What's love
got to do with it? The thought of Agnes's tongue
picking its way across José's body like a mother chimp

delousing her brat ceases to burn, and now his brain
is left vaguely purified. Into this empty space
each of Agnes's faults steps up to fill the void—
how she slurps her soup and makes him lower

the toilet seat. As for José, he's a cipher, a prick
on wheels. These outbursts of clarity that reach us
when it's almost too late—the precision of vision
of the man on the gallows as the trap springs open,

the articulation begun in wisdom and ending in a yelp,
perhaps only here is reason to be found. Stuck above
the roar of buses our friend on the ledge might be
the world's wisest man were it not for the acrophobic

scream in his brain. Here we have him at his best.
Will it last? Regrettably, with each tiptoe and terror-
packed step back toward his balcony his muddy thinking
reasserts itself, until when he reaches safety his only

thought is of José clamped to his beloved's body
like a pit bull on a chew toy. Moments later, when
he rushes to Agnes's apartment to beat upon the door,
the single residual scrap of newly grasped wisdom

is Do what you want but avoid heights. A Socrates
above the street, once in his living room he reverts
to the rank and file that includes us all. As for
his recent folly, he sees it as sacrifice: the gift of what

he had done being like a diamond ring, the absolute
proof that it's his sweetheart's duty to love him back.
The door flies open and it's José who doesn't get
these niceties of self-deception and knocks him flat.

TOO MUCH SKEPTICISM IS LIKE A PUNCH TO THE HEAD

Matthew 21, 19

A fig tree thinking fig-tree thoughts, growing
by the side of the road, with its metaphorical hands
deep in its fig-tree pockets, when the lord comes along
with his companions in righteousness, a very phalanx

of correction. All day the lord has been lecturing
the local folk on the wages of sin and his throat is parched.
Give me a fig, he demands. But the tree has none left.
The last he gave to a beggar, the one before that

to a child with one leg. The tree shrugs its shoulders,
a Hebrew gesture. The companions gasp. The lord
lifts his staff and curses the tree from its top branch
to its deepest root. Then the lord and his henchmen

trudge off through the dust to their next miracle.
Like a defeated boxer at the end of a lackluster career,
the fig tree spends years trembling all over before
it can squeeze out even the smallest fig—a cross

between a walnut and a prune, and by then the lord
is history. These are the famous Yesbut figs renowned
throughout the Near East. For instance, a famous
Aramaic preacher speaks of the lord's great kindness.

The fig tree says, Yesbut. An early Christian saint
strolls by singing the lord's praises. Yesbut, says the tree.
The figs are prized by Stoic philosophers, pagan healers,
alchemists, heretic confabulators, poets. Even today

one might slip into the market by mistake—tough-skinned
with a spicy, blotting-paper taste. Try taking a small bite.
Do you see how the sun fades and storm clouds threaten?
You weep a little and the world's promises waver like

heat lines on a desert horizon. These figs—what problems
they cause. Quick. Throw the rest in the trash. Now wipe
your eyes, put on your nightshirt, creep off to bed. At dawn
when you wake your dreams will have reknit themselves.

For breakfast eat a pomegranate and a few plump grapes—
those fruits brought to Moses out of the Promised Land—
then nibble an apple from the almighty's original Garden,
soothing produce with respectable histories. Once more

the day begins to smile. Not real, of course, but enough
to help you forget your sadness, put aside your doubts.
Already you feel better. Yes, but, you argue, yes, but. . . .
No buts about it, your dream of the world whispers back.

FOR THOSE WHOSE MOUTHS ARE PACKED
WITH SUCKLING PIG

It's hard to be the conscience of the suburban streets,
selling hunger to the well fed. The glad-bellies
fix their eyes on the empty plate and say, What's

that? Like Virgin Birth, quarks or pissing up a rope,
it's a trick to wrap the mind around, especially
for those who never fret if life exists past lunch.

So this oldster in torn robes and rope-soled shoes,
after a day of warning householders of the wages of sin
and imminent doom, when the sun goes down, he sighs

and takes a taxi home. Here he strips off his costume
to reveal that underneath he's a young guy after all—
a handsome pilgrim with a burning sense of mission.

But what does it take to get his message across?
Bleeding wounds, a troop of lepers? After dinner
as his kids watch TV and his wife complains

about the bills, our friend repaints his signs
with brighter colors and tries to get each threat
exactly right. What a waste of time, we think—

except his warnings make our food taste sweeter.
But despite his aching heart, he can't sustain the pace.
The strain's too great, and faced with mounting debt

he is forced to seek out other work. By summer,
in a clean white suit and wearing an approximation
of a smile, he peddles ice cream along these streets

where once he menaced all with hell. But has he
truly changed his spots? For at times, like a message
in a fortune cookie, a customer will find scrawled

across a Popsicle stick the words, You Must Repent;
or within the rum raisin or tutti-frutti, he'll discover
a clove of garlic, a shot of vinegar, hot red peppers.

PUNISHMENTS

after T. Lux

Bad rat, tied to a stake, actually
a column, maybe Corinthian. Bad rat,
erect on two feet, paws behind your back,
two bags of grain swing from your jaws,

two fat tiny sacks joined together
by a hank of rope. Bad rat, you must have been
vexatious, you must have been a crook.
Did you snitch the grain, you cretin?

What a bit of cheap deceit. Then why
do you smirk? Even bound to a stake,
you appear sardonic, a trifle lack-
adaisical. All this is a sketch cut

into gold, the flat surface of a ring
worn by a Greek lady in Alexandria,
three centuries before Christ, who said
nothing of note on the subject of rats.

Bad rat, you should have let the grain alone.
You should have eaten green, green grass.
You should have snacked on twigs. Bad rat
eats grain. Bad lion eats sheep. Bad hawk

snatches a rabbit. Bad fish eats a smaller fish.
And me, a gatherer of words, a slinger
of words, I spoke too many, slung too many.
Bow your head, step to the stake. Bad rat.

THE LAST TAKE-OUT SUPPER

Jesus agreed to send out for Chinese.
Styrofoam containers were placed before
the Disciples. All received two egg rolls.
Mark taught Luke how to work the chopsticks.
James overturned his hot and sour soup.
Matthew and John each got one wonton.
Thomas wouldn't share his mu-shoo pork.
As typically happens, the rice was cold,
the tea boiling hot. Simon burned his tongue.
Jesus made brief remarks about the future.
Peter received a fortune but no cookie.
Judas got a cookie without a fortune.
Outside, the soldiers marched past unheard—
often the case when one is having fun.

A MORNING PRE-BEEF

Draped along the electric fence, the meadow's
unkempt forsythia brags Krugerrand yellow
upon this balmy April morning. Sparrows
are all aflutter and the dozen Jersey cows

mutter, Hot damn, hot damn, but very
slowly; pokier in fact than their relaxed
mastication of newly sprouted grass, so sweet,
so good. Can't we spot a cow's felicity

in the quality of tail-flick, the vigorous
evacuation of cow plop? Bluebottle flies
swarm helter-skelter over its bronze surface

like hooky-playing boys on the first warm day
at the beach, while even a mechanism as mean
as the gut-wrenching electric fence, hums.

COLD NIGHTS

Some nights sitting alone in a café
or taking a break in his backyard
in late summer with the wind jostling
the day lilies, as evening starts to fall,

the man sees with perfect clarity
how his future will unwind without
the maybes and sugary what ifs—
the impossible check that could arrive,

or the college friend from Cleveland
who might call about a job. Like taking
a picture from his wallet that brings
to mind each detail of a special day,

a house he'd rented on the Cape in July
with his friends all gathered around,
but the reverse, the dark side of what
had been light, all the sharply detailed

and irreversible declines. It's not
a place to stay for long. Put it away.
Let's think of something else. Now
it flips upside down and the man becomes

like someone who wakes in the night
to find the window open and his blankets
tumbled to the floor, and still half-asleep
he drags them up, pulls them to his chin.

What was that dream of the rented house
and his friends spread out across the lawn—
laughter and the click of croquet balls,
shafts of yellow light through the pines?

COUNTRY CLUB

Among the yellow leaves of old oaks,
six Canada geese parade as stately
as dowagers in feathered coats
across the golf course in single file.

This is my sixty-first autumn,
and binding me more tightly each year
is the garment made of all the years before.
Is there nothing without its fixed point

on the line of cause and effect, nothing
without some history being dragged
along behind? Geese, grass and trees,
I see them through the filter of sixty

previous landscapes. A green golf cart
with two men in bright yellow slacks
rounds a nearby oak and stops. Spreading
its wings, the lead goose rears up; but

intent on their game, the men don't notice.
To own a thing is to try to freeze it in time.
Feeling certain that all this belongs to them,
the men swing their clubs at the little white ball.

Autumn, autumn, how many will follow?
My sense of wonder is as thin as an old sheet
washed over and over; my sense of consequence
fattens above me, feathered and huge.

POEM ENDING WITH A LINE BY SU TUNG-PO

My friend is afraid he is dying. Of course,
he has always known this, but now the procedure
has gotten faster. How to ignore a subject
when it persists in forcing its dark mass
against the brain.
                    Cracked mufflers versus Bach:
one struggles to admire the delicacy of the partita
as traffic squalor pushes through the open window.

Ahead waits a dark night with a single star.
Behind extends the long view down the mountain.
Should I regret my death if it is inevitable?
Should I regret my life if it is always passing?
How to be both arrow and bow.
                    Released, the arrow
flies past the dead oak at the end of the path.
One must make certain the mind never clings.

for Hayden Carruth

WHAT HAD SEEMED PERMANENT

Each morning at daybreak the small beagle
crossed the road to the barn, where a neighbor
milked her cows, to demand his ritual bowl

of milk. He had his whole day planned out.
Now, forty years later, the dog's a memory,
the cows have gone, the neighbor's past ninety;

yet on a nail in the barn hangs the dog's collar,
while nearby a few milk cans remain. And deep
in the woods I often spot cellar holes, almost

overgrown, close to the graveyard of a family
that lasted several generations, digging rocks
from the New Hampshire dirt, and then died out

or headed west. Each summer treasure hunters
with metal detectors unearth coins, old spoons,
displaying their finds at the Columbus Day fair.

Today I see them there—the oddments left behind—
rings, a tarnished cup with half a name, a locket
with a blurred face—gifts that had once seemed

permanent. From the crowded midway, I hear
the music of a dozen rides, a discordant jangle,
where couples, in a circular whip, are sent careening

into autumn air. The view from the top must snatch
their breath as fall color spreads all its variations
up the mountain toward winter. Reaching the peak

of their arc before they plummet to apparent death,
the couples scream. How eagerly they play at chaos,
before stumbling back to the day's brief immortality.

THOMAS THE DOUBTER'S IRREFUTABLE CHINK

One fat finger shoved through the skin's pink slit,
the rosy folds of which seem to grasp the tip
of this worker's mitt, toughened, gray with dirt,
but nonetheless poked through the delicate cleft,

a minor rape, but well recalled and one in which
I would have gladly partook, would have crammed
my fingers in there too, having washed them first,
would have shoved them deep, then wiggled them.

In Caravaggio's painting, Christ pulls back his clothing,
even assists Thomas, grips his wrist, pushes his finger
into the wound beneath Christ's breast. Thomas bends,
wide-eyed, his brow a snake-nest of wrinkles. Matthew

and Mark, no skeptics themselves, are struck dumb
despite their best intentions and start to pick the words
with which to later write it down. Christ seems calm,
but ill at ease, as one might with a finger on your lung.

What a marvelous story. Twelve disciples: nine hotshots,
a traitor, a doubter and Peter the waffler, but Thomas
looks like the only one having fun, happily aghast,
nudging his lord's innards through the spear-shaped cut

where the Roman soldier guessed he'd polished off the job.
Trust me when I say that before this moment the word
flabbergasted didn't exist. Who wouldn't have jumped
to stick a finger down that irrefutable chink? I'd have

kicked and bit. And then came the tall tales: a string
of embellishments passed on from one nutcase to the next
and winding up as joke like this. But the chance to poke
a digit deep in the lord's gut—Thomas had all the luck.

WHAT HE HAD BEEN PROMISED

Here was my portion: the most beautiful women,
bravest heroes, powerful kings and queens
to fetch and flit as chattel at my command,
to flatter and serve as my compliant population—
and this was true and all were dead.

I hadn't thought to mind the lack of weather,
the disfigured landscape, to suffer the isolation.
In grief, the dead lack all gift of conversation.
They do no more than whine. Was there honor
in parading as their god?

At times in my hunger I'd choose a companion.
You will see the sort of humiliations I endured.
I'd pick from the women whomever I desired
and force her icy thighs in a joyless fornication
where I was briefly held.

At last I hunted elsewhere. Surely, it was absurd
to think I might have won the favor of any woman
but a half-wit or saint. Tricked by her living passion,
I carried off a woman who was mad.
Kiss me, kiss me—I am cold.

AIDONEUS—HADES—UNSEEN ONE

Poppies with my own hands I had sown
along the banks of the river of sadness,
then an old guy to ferry the dead for a price.
I thought she'd grin at how the poor had to swim.

For her pleasure alone I planted fields of asphodel
where the dead, their memories gone, had to present
an amusing ballet, mimicking each moment
of their mortal span, not knowing this was hell.

Nothing relieved her dejection. Yet in six months,
as the day came for our parting, her face brightened
like her absent sun, as I prepared to be abandoned.

What good is love when the rest is not enough?
The gags and pratfalls, my carnival of the absurd—
not once did she laugh at my three-headed dog.

THE CAT WITH ITS TOYS

Already she has convinced you of my deception.
Her suffering and return home every six months—
you like these honeyed versions of her abduction.

It was her pallor that first drew my attention:
the pallor of death, the odor of damp earth—
birth and growing things, she said—her own deception.

But about her smell and pallor I wasn't mistaken.
She was eager to leave the boredom of her former life,
despite a show of grief, her version of her abduction.

Soon she grew obsessed with the ways of ruination,
while I felt not being on Earth was penalty enough,
but already she has convinced you of my deception.

Mocking my attempts to direct her education,
she mastered all the ways of torture, outdoing Death
in cruelty. Yet you prefer her version of the abduction.

Was it that she lacked brute strength, that as a woman
deceit became the tool of her ambition? I waste my breath:
already she has convinced you of my deception
with her false and honeyed versions of the abduction.

PLUTO

Afraid to name me, the living named me Wealth,
for perhaps they saw that wealth was what I was,
since of the two divisions, the quick and the dead,

mine was by far the larger. As for the living's time
on Earth, how could such a minor fluttering equal
their duration in my kingdom? So these were riches

of a sort. And their grief on arriving in my realm,
it too was short-lived. They grew used to death
simply by forgetting—like a man who can't recall

a name or date. It's on the tip of my tongue, he says,
thinking it will spring to mind. What was the last
thing I did and what happened before that? And so

he reenacts each moment of his life but nothing
helps and his confusion lengthens into forever.
Such is my offered bliss. But he's not unhappy;

he lacks the gift to be unhappy. So if the living
call me Wealth, fearing that another name—Doom,
Destiny or Damnation—might encourage me

to snatch them up too soon, they fail to grasp
my wealth is merely their accumulated memory.
As for their present habitation, I am caretaker only.

Down to their last cry has their time been measured.
I do no more than welcome. But powerless themselves,
it cheers the living to think they have a scrap of power,

able to fight or run, whine or argue before their string
is cut and they set out on their long release with a vague
look of wonder and a stray memory just beyond reach.

SMALL

Giovanni Bellini painted till ninety
a biblical variety including about forty
Virgins and Child at his art factory

in Venice. In one, a redheaded toddler
raises his hand both in blessing and warning,
balloon-faced and standing on a blue cloak

draped across the Virgin's lap. He doesn't doubt
the day's solemnity, nor does the Virgin, though
a touch of worry eases her religious austerity—

human concern arising from Number One Mom—
and she hopes for the best, since the gesture,
really, is meant for us; that either we get

with the program or face a hereafter packed
with regret. Maybe a certain frivolity is being
held against us, or a shared brutality evolving

from spite, envy, the usual causes, as once again
our faults are evoked—Carp, carp, but nicely put.
On either side of the central scene, a rustic

landscape retreats to a castle-topped mountain
as clouds meander through an otherwise blue sky.
To the left we glimpse a farm, then a monastery

nestled beneath the hillside's sudden climb.
To the right a shepherd reclines with his lambs
under a bridge, as a monk on horseback trots

toward the monastery, which, I expect, he hopes
to reach before lunch. Despite the Virgin's worry
it's a nice day in sunny Italy, as life displays

its quotidian pleasures. Perhaps Bellini felt torn
by his central theme—no threat seems to lurk
and the lambs appear free from a future made up

of stew, roast or chops. The horse goes clippity-clop,
its orderly progression being contentment's temporal
embodiment. Time creeps ahead. Then from the horse

there drops a turd and the sun glistens on its golden
flakings. Far below two ants glance up. Who knows
what they think? The moment keeps its mystery,

but remains upbeat. All is light, impossible light,
and the ants, in the companionable way of their kind,
bump shoulders once or twice and pass on.

For Carl Dennis

THREE CHRISTS OF YPSILANTI

Rotten apples in a barrel, how many
before you toss them out? Take
the Last Supper. Do you recollect
the fresco by Leonardo: eleven jittery

customers and one with a guilty smirk?
Jesus has just said, "One of you will
soon betray me," and his Disciples
are choking on their bread sticks.

Of course they recover. After all, Jesus
needed an accuser. "What you must do,
do quickly," he told Judas. But what if two,
four or six had done the double-cross?

When do you decide to discard the lot?
When does Jesus make up his mind
to forget the deity racket and rejoin
his step-pop in the carpenter shop?

What if all twelve had run to the cops
to demand their bag of silver, leaving
Jesus with the leftovers and dirty plates?
Would he still accept the crucifixion

and march gladly up Golgotha? And
has this happened? How many heroes
have been dragged to jail or the hatch
when their disciples at last determined

they must be nuts? Messiahs pack asylums
like fleas crowd a dog. In fact, how lucky
to have just a single Judas in our lives.
But I prefer the other ones, the saviors

who lost twelve out of twelve, but kept
trying to lug their burdens up the mountain.
Instead they got tossed into institutions.
One's in a dungeon preaching to the ants,

another uses a tack to chip his life story
into a brick, a third shouts about being
forsaken, but he can't recall by whom.
Was it you or you? Water drips—blip, blip—

a noise resembling speech. Our victim
grows alert. How I delight in the human!
Faced with nothingness or a friendly ear,
he'll soon be hearing voices even here.

MYSTERY, SO LONG

At first, it filled the space around us with holes,
the mystery. It was scary. People fell through them.
There goes Og, people might say. They sang hymns
to the mystery. They pounded on drums. They fed
the mystery both friends and strangers. It seemed

a good idea. The mystery hungered for human flesh.
Oh, implacable and mysterious mystery.
But bit by bit people started patching over the holes—
first with mud and sticks, then with bricks and mortar.
You get the idea. Some holes vanished, others got smaller.

Time passed. The mystery stopped being such a big deal.
As for the last holes, people knew their time was coming.
Scientists still got excited, but politicians began playing golf.
The mystery started to disappear, just as giants and ogres
had disappeared—the ones who had terrified villages,

wore animal skins and never washed. They had kept
getting smaller until they were nearly indistinguishable
from homeless people, living in alleys or under bridges.
In the winter they went to Phoenix or Tampa, warm places.
The only people they continued to frighten were children,

until their mothers told them not to stare—the mystery
was like that: unwashed and undependable, a security risk.
My neighbor complains, My car won't start, it's a mystery.
My friend scratches his head, My wife left me, it's a mystery.
Sometimes it's a mystery why I don't hurt myself laughing.

This morning I'm stuck in traffic—for miles extends a mass
of parked cars. I don't know what's wrong; it's a mystery.
Then up above a biplane begins to shoot out puffs of smoke
into the immaculate blue sky: an emissary from yesterday
offering hope for tomorrow. These sweet cottony morsels,

their tender solicitude nearly breaks my heart. In seconds
will come the head-slapping sense of defeat, but not yet.
What is the balance between too much mystery and too little?
Harry's Hash House for Tired Travelers. We lurch forward.
Cars fender bender each other into an unconditional future.

FIELD NOTES ON DIVINE EVOLUTION

The first gods said Er and I beg your pardon;
they tapped people on the shoulder, people
who wore the skins of saber-toothed tigers,

if they wore anything at all. The first gods
were bigger than people, but not big enough
to be frightening. They would say, Hey, look

at that tree, I just made it. What do you think?
The people would criticize the tree, or yawn
and walk away. It was like that all the time.

The next gods decided right off the bat not to be
pushovers. They invented thunder and lightning.
They made floods and enjoyed seeing people run.

They sat on mountaintops and watched people
run to the north, then run even faster to the south.
People grew weak with fatigue. They slept more

and never out in the open. They kept apologizing
and blaming one another. My neighbor did it;
I saw him—people said stuff like that every day.

The gods who came next were very different.
Whatever you have done or will do, they said,
you're already forgiven. People came to a stop.

They wanted it repeated. Forgiven, said the gods,
Good or bad, beautiful or ugly, you're off the hook.
They put a few mortals in charge to make sure

it was done right. But it's hard to be in charge
when everybody has already been forgiven.
It seemed reckless to forgive even the bad people

or the people who looked like they'd be bad soon.
Shortly it was necessary to change the conditions:
You are forgiven if you do this; you are forgiven

if you do that. As for forgiveness pure and simple,
it was like a lion among schoolchildren: too risky
to be set loose. When the last group of gods arrived,

they were skeptical. They walked around the people
and rolled their eyes. Not all were critical, but none
were enthusiastic. They frowned and scuffed their feet.

Soon they wandered off to pursue their discussions—
whether we have value, our mix of virtues and faults,
whether there was reason to keep up the relationship.

You ask about their language? They speak in colors.
At times the scrap of a single word, perhaps no more
than the equivalent of a letter, may be briefly visible,

but paler, a truncated shadow after traveling so far.
We see it arcing through the sky after a summer rain—
encouraging evidence their debate still continues.

THE CUNNING ONE

It happened like this: he lived in a palace
that was also a prison. You understand
how nothing is ever simple. He had built
a labyrinth for the king's monster son,

a great service, which came with a secret.
One for the king, one in the builder's head.
Be reasonable, could the king ever permit him
to return to the easy conversations of Athens?

But because the king was grateful, no luxury
was spared in the palace which was also
a prison. Wherever one turned, one found
beauty and opulence. Gorgeous wall hangings,

thick rugs, soft cushions. All entertainments
were prepared for him, from the scholarly
to the perverse: the moist flesh of children,
stimulants to engender the sweetest dreams.

Still, the door was locked and after he had walked
through the rooms and saw what was to be seen,
he ripped apart the feather cushions and made
himself a pair of wings. By morning he was gone.

How we love these stories. Think of Adam and Eve,
wasn't the Garden for them a similar prison?
And Satan, once he foresaw an eternity of Heaven's
coercive beauty, what could he do but rebel?

ARTIST

A knot of string, crossed sticks, a dab of ink—
can't any work begin as a passionate doodling?
So here is another of his constructions: a wooden

cow, but so skillful even the bull was tricked.
You see, one must reckon with the jaded boredom
of queens. During the drawn-out days, she lusted

for the bull. What was he? Beef on the hoof,
nothing special. But she stood at the fence
and watched the bull's prick—its muscularity,

its obscene forcefulness—until she couldn't live
without that dazzle within her. So she went
to the artist and he made a cow that the queen

could hide herself within. The bull mounted
the cow, but it was the woman, her aroused wetness.
And the artist? Can he be blamed for the ends

for which he used his gift? He was the maker.
It was his sickness. It masked what was made.
Consider this, he never heard her brute moaning.

DISCORD

Never ignore what began his wanderings.
In Athens he was the greatest craftsman,
with so much work he had to hire his nephew
to help him. But his nephew had his gift

and soon people claimed the nephew's gift
was greater than the uncle's. If the uncle
built with bronze, the nephew built with gold.
And so his uncle's resentment and envy grew,

until at last he killed him, who also loved him.
You see, he had no choice. To be outdone
meant to accept his own ruin. For this murder
he was banished from his homeland. But he

had not counted on the arguments of the dead,
how they hold the last word on all subjects.
He would make the statue of a god or a bauble
for a queen, and then lift it up to the specter

of his nephew. See this? he would say. Could
you ever make this? And of course the nephew
was silent, itself an answer: the better answer.
The uncle worked harder, statues and buildings

became grander and the uncle's traveling
was ceaseless. He became known as the greatest
of all craftsmen. But you understand how fate
can trick you. Without his nephew's murder,

he wouldn't have become famous, yet no joy
could he take in any of his marvels—temple,
toy or statue—when in its glossy surfaces
he kept confronting the dead face he loved.

ICARUS'S FLIGHT

What else could the boy have done? Wasn't
flight both an escape and a great uplifting?
And so he flew. But how could he appreciate
his freedom without knowing the exact point

where freedom stopped? So he flew upward
and the sun dissolved the wax and he fell.
But at least in his anticipated plummeting
he grasped the confines of what had been

his liberty. You think he flew too far?
He flew just far enough. He flew precisely
to the point of wisdom. Would it
have been better to flutter ignorantly

from petal to petal within some garden
forever? As a result, flight for him was not
upward escape, but descent, with his wings
disintegrating around him. Should it matter

that neither shepherd nor farmer with his plow
watched him fall? He now had his answer,
laws to uphold him in his downward plunge.
Cushion enough for what he wanted.

BLEMISHED AND UNBLEMISHED

Say genius is one side of the mountain,
is vanity the other? Think of Daedalus
after he escaped from the king's prison.
The king pursued him. He had many jewels

but Daedalus was brightest. Of course
Daedalus concealed himself. The king went
to his lesser kings and set them a task.
He gave each a spiral shell and told them

to run a thread through the spiral, a tiny
labyrinth, much like the one that Daedalus
had made for the king. And one after another
the lesser kings failed at this task.

The great king came to Daedalus's protector
and set him the same task. Of course he couldn't
resolve it. So he presented it to Daedalus,
who guessed the reason for the puzzle,

that he was the only person who could
understand it and this was how the king
had determined to trap him. Still, Daedalus
couldn't keep himself from the solution.

He pricked a tiny hole in one end of the shell
and covered it with a drop of honey. Then he
fixed a gossamer thread to the leg of an ant
and the ant wound its way through the labyrinth

to the sweetness. But it wasn't enough simply
to solve the problem; it was also necessary
that the solution be known. So he gave the shell
to his protector, who presented it to the king,

who demanded that Daedalus be returned to him.
The protector refused and in the following battle
many were killed, including the king himself,
who had once been Daedalus's friend. Is this

what makes art important to us? The paradox
that the flawlessness of the work is fashioned
from the mass of human failings? Here is vanity,
here gluttony, here lust and murder—but polished,

with the sting of our imperfections blunted,
the bloody stain washed out. Art bears witness
to the possibility of perfection. Not for us
but for what is made: white silks from muddy paws.

LAST WISDOM

So often in this world what is rejected
crawls back to the heart, what is cast off
again crowds the brain. Think of Daedalus,
at the end of his life, gone to Sardinia

as builder for the son of Heracles. But faces
fretted his memory and he began to make
bronze dolls with movable limbs, forming
their faces into the faces he once loved.

Here was the son who tumbled into the sea,
here the beloved wife long dead, the sister
who hanged herself, the nephew he murdered,
the great king he had betrayed. And others,

their shapes filled his room. He clothed them
and put hair on their heads. He placed small
devices in their hearts so they could walk
and lift their arms. They grouped around him,

but remained silent. Hoping to make them talk,
he plucked out the tongues of birds and crafted
stringed boxes through which the air swirled
to create a wailing, but still the creatures

wouldn't speak. So Daedalus disguised his voice,
making it like a woman's, then a boy's. Forgiven,
he said, you are forgiven. And the dolls jittered
their arms. But when people passing on the street

heard him call out, they jeered at him. You see
his gift stopped short of what he wanted most.
You are forgiven, he shouted to the dumb things.
But he spoke falsely. His trinkets gave no relief.

Was this the wisdom to come to him last?
That nothing could rid him of his isolation?
His toys no longer hid what was there: himself
and the night and the only entry into night.

ACKNOWLEDGMENTS

Many thanks are due to the editors of the following
publications, in which this work first appeared.

The American Poetry Review: "THE BALANCE," "DANCE, DANCE,"
"FUNCTIONAL FORGETTING," 'LEARNING TO COPE," "TOWARD SOME
BRIGHT MOMENT," and "UNEXPECTED HOLIDAY."
Darksun: "AT HOME WITH ANGELS" and "SCOFFLAW."
The Georgia Review: "DO THEY HAVE A REASON."
The Greensboro Review: "AN ARTIST LIKE ANY OTHER,"
"THE PIG'S COMPLAINT TO HIS QUEEN," "SAYING NO," and
"FOR THOSE WHOSE MOUTHS ARE PACKED WITH SUCKLING PIG."
The Green Mountain Review: "TOO MUCH SKEPTICISM IS
LIKE A PUNCH TO THE HEAD."
Lumina: "CHUCKLEHEADS."
Marlborough Review: "BAD RAT," "DRIVING PAST THE BRIDGE," and
"LIVING IN A NICE PLACE."
The New Yorker: "THE BIRTH OF ANGELS," "COUNTRY CLUB," and
"JONAH'S FLIGHT TO TARSHISH."
Ninth Letter: "COLD NIGHTS," "ODDS AND ENDS," and "WHAT HAD
SEEMED PERMANENT."
Ploughshares: "ARTIST," "BLEMISHED AND UNBLEMISHED,"
"THE CUNNING ONE," "DISCORD," "ICARUS'S FLIGHT," and
"LAST WISDOM."
Poetry: "ALLIGATOR DARK," "DEAD ROPE," "PENNY FOR YOUR
THOUGHTS," "THE MERCY OF LAZARUS," "NO MOMENT PAST THIS
ONE," "POEM ENDING WITH A LINE BY SU TUNG-PO," and
"THE SIDEBOARD'S MAHOGANY SURFACE."
The Poetry Society: "THE APPRECIATION OF BEAUTY."
Rattle: "HIDE AND SEEK" and "MYSTERY, SO LONG."
Terminus: "HACK WORK," "OLD FARTS' BALL," and
"THE LAST TAKE-OUT SUPPER."
Triquarterly Review: "THE SACRIFICE," "THREE CHRISTS OF YPSILANTI,"
and "THOMAS THE DOUBTER'S IRREFUTABLE CHINK."

ABOUT THE AUTHOR

Stephen Dobyns has published eleven prior books of poetry and twenty novels, including ten mystery novels set in Saratoga Springs. His first book of poems, *Concurring Beasts,* was the Lamont Poetry Selection of the Academy of American Poets for 1972. *Black Dog, Red Dog* was a winner in the National Poetry Series. *Cemetery Nights* won the Poetry Society of America's Melville Cane Award in 1987. Dobyns has received a Guggenheim and three fellowships from the National Endowment of the Arts. The second and expanded edition of his book of essays on poetry, *Best Words, Best Order,* appeared in 2002. His most recent book of fiction is a collection of stories, *Eating Naked* (2000). His most recent book of poetry is *The Porcupine's Kisses* (2002). Dobyns lives in Westerly, Rhode Island. He teaches in the MFA programs at Warren Wilson and Sarah Lawrence colleges.

PENGUIN POETS

TED BERRIGAN
Selected Poems
The Sonnets

PHILIP BOOTH
Lifelines

JIM CARROLL
Fear of Dreaming
Void of Course

BARBARA CULLY
Desire Reclining

CARL DENNIS
New and Selected
Poems 1974–2004
Practical Gods

DIANE DI PRIMA
Loba

STUART DISCHELL
Dig Safe

STEPHEN DOBYNS
Mystery, So Long
Pallbearers Envying
the One Who Rides
The Porcupine's Kisses

ROGER FANNING
Homesick

AMY GERSTLER
Crown of Weeds
Ghost Girl
Medicine
Nerve Storm

DEBORA GREGER
Desert Fathers,
Uranium Daughters
God
Western Art

ROBERT HUNTER
Sentinel

BARBARA JORDAN
Trace Elements

MARY KARR
Viper Rum

JACK KEROUAC
Book of Blues
Book of Haikus

JOANNE KYGER
As Ever

ANN LAUTERBACH
Hum
If in Time
On a Stair

PHILLIS LEVIN
Mercury

WILLIAM LOGAN
Macbeth in Venice
Night Battle
Vain Empires

DEREK MAHON
Selected Poems

MICHAEL MCCLURE
Huge Dreams: San
Francisco and Beat
Poems

CAROL MUSKE
An Octave Above
Thunder

ALICE NOTLEY
The Descent of Alette
Disobedience
Mysteries of Small
Houses

LAWRENCE RAAB
The Probable World
Visible Signs

PATTIANN ROGERS
Generations

STEPHANIE
STRICKLAND
V

ANNE WALDMAN
Kill or Cure
Marriage: A Sentence
Structure of the World
Compared to a
Bubble

JAMES WELCH
Riding the
Earthboy 40

PHILIP WHALEN
Overtime: Selected
Poems

ROBERT WRIGLEY
Lives of the Animals
Reign of Snakes

JOHN YAU
Borrowed Love Poems